The Hangman

LOUISE PENNY

The Hangman

Grass Roots Press

First published in 2010 by Grass Roots Press

The Good Reads series is funded in part by the Government of Canada's Office of Literacy and Essential Skills.

Grass Roots Press also gratefully acknowledges the financial support for its publishing programs provided by the following agencies: the Government of Canada through the Canada Book Fund and the Government of Alberta through the Alberta Foundation for the Arts. 　Foundation for the Arts

Grass Roots Press would also like to thank ABC Life Literacy Canada for their support. Good Reads® is used under licence from ABC Life Literacy Canada.

Library and Archives Canada Cataloguing in Publication

Penny, Louise
　　The hangman / Louise Penny.

(Good reads series)
ISBN 978-1-771533-83-6

　　1. Readers for new literates. I. Title. II. Series: Good reads series (Edmonton, Alta.)

PS8631.E572H35 2010　　　428.6'2　　　C2010-901986-5

For my mother, Barbara,
who read to me

Chapter One

Armand Gamache didn't like what he was looking at, but then, few people would.

"I don't see a note, chief," Inspector Beauvoir reported. He was searching the ground.

"Keep looking, please," said Chief Inspector Gamache. "It might have blown away."

All around him his police team was hard at work, taking pictures, taking samples, putting out police tape.

"Crime scene," the bright yellow plastic tape said.

But was it a crime scene?

While his team was busy, Chief Inspector Gamache was still and silent, like the forest itself. They were deep in the woods of Quebec this November morning. The chief felt the cold and damp. He pulled his coat closer, trying to find some warmth. But there was little warmth and no comfort to be found.

A man was hanging from a tree in front of him.

Gamache tore his eyes from the body and looked at the tree. It, too, looked dead. Its leaves were brown and dry. The branches clacked together in the wind like bones.

What a terrible place to end a life, he thought. Why would someone choose to die here?

Gamache turned back to the dead man. He was middle-aged, with greying hair. He wore a warm coat, but his hat lay on the ground below him.

Did it make sense to dress warmly to kill yourself?

Did this poor man take his own life? Gamache wondered. Or was it taken from him?

Had he been murdered?

"Dr. Harris is here." Inspector Beauvoir pointed to a woman following one of the police officers through the woods.

"Doctor." He greeted her with a small bow, then stood aside.

The doctor saw why she was there. She had never gotten used to violent death, though she saw it almost every day. It still made her sad. That was one of the many things she liked about Chief Inspector Gamache. Death also made him sad. He never joked in the company of the dead. Never made fun.

This was not funny.

"When was he found?" Dr. Harris asked as they walked closer to the hanged man. She tried not to think of him as just a body. It was important not to forget that this thing strung up from the tree had once felt as they did. Had once held a lover's hand. Had once smiled at a child. Had once had dreams. And sorrows.

What sorrow had brought him here? To this tree and to this end?

"He was found about two hours ago," said Gamache, and pointed to a man wrapped in a blanket. "By that man over there."

"A jogger?" Dr. Harris asked. The man was wearing a sweat suit and running shoes.

Inspector Beauvoir nodded. "He's staying at the local Inn and Spa. Name is Tom Scott. He found the man at seven-thirty this morning and called the police."

"Do we know who the dead man is?"

"Not yet, but Mr. Scott thinks he may know the man. It's hard to say for sure."

Dr. Harris nodded. She doubted that the dead man's mother would know him right away. Hanging did that to a person's face.

"Scott didn't try to cut him down?" she asked.

Chief Inspector Gamache shook his head. "No. He told the officers he didn't have a knife."

Gamache knew that was reasonable. Who went jogging with a knife? Except maybe in Detroit. And even then the weapon would be a gun. And the person would be running more than jogging.

But he also knew the doctor had hit on one very troubling part of this sad event. Why hadn't Tom Scott tried to help the man? It would be natural to at least try to do something. And yet he'd done nothing.

Chapter Two

Dr. Harris and Inspector Beauvoir watched the dead man being lowered to the ground. At the same time, Chief Inspector Gamache walked over to the living man. Tom Scott.

"How are you feeling?"

"Sick and cold. Can I go now?"

"In a minute."

"I've been here for hours." Tom Scott looked at his watch. "It's almost ten. I've missed breakfast. My wife will kill me."

"Perhaps you should call her."

Scott paused. "That's okay."

"I insist. I wouldn't want her to worry."

"I already called. She's fine."

Seeing Gamache's face, he said in a small voice, "This is my vacation. I don't get many. I just want to get back to the Inn."

"Tell me again what happened."

Tom Scott took a deep breath. "I woke up early, and it was a nice day, so I decided to go for a jog. The woman at the front desk said there were paths cut through the woods where I could run. So I did. After about five minutes, I found . . ." He jerked his head toward the now-empty tree.

"What did you do?"

"I had my cell phone with me, so I called the police. Then I called my wife."

Gamache studied Tom Scott. He was lying. That much was certain. But why? What was this nervous little man hiding?

"And then what did you do?"

"I waited for the cops. What else would I do? Keep on jogging?"

"You might have tried to help the man."

"Are you crazy?" Scott yelled. "Did you see what he looked like? You should thank me for even stopping and calling. I could have just run away. But I didn't."

Scott was so angry he trembled.

The chief inspector waited. And waited. Quietly staring at Tom Scott.

"What?" Scott's voice was high, like a girl's. "What is it?"

"You might have helped the man," Gamache said again.

"He was dead!"

"He certainly was by the time we arrived."

"What are you saying?" Scott's face went from red to white. "That I had something to do with this?"

Armand Gamache said nothing. He knew that screaming and yelling upset people. But silence was even more disturbing.

"Tell me the truth, Mr. Scott," the chief inspector's voice was calm but commanding. Here was a man used to leading and used to being followed.

"I am." Tom Scott dropped his eyes to the dead leaves on the ground. A few feet away lay the dead man. The earth seemed covered in death.

Gamache decided to drop the subject and move to another topic.

"You told one of my officers that the man looked familiar. Where did you see him?"

"The Inn. I think he might be one of the guests."

"Chief?" Inspector Beauvoir waved. He and Dr. Harris were kneeling over the body.

"Excuse me," Gamache said, and walked over. "What have you found?"

He knelt to join them.

"He's been dead since last night, probably since early evening," said Dr. Harris. "Say, seven or eight o'clock. Hanged himself with medium-weight rope. His neck is broken. I suspect he climbed to the second branch, tied the rope on, then tied it around his neck."

"And threw himself off," said Inspector Beauvoir.

The chief inspector looked down at the dead man's face. What despair had driven him to kill himself? And in this terrible way?

"Would his death have been fast?"

"Very," said Dr. Harris.

That was something, the chief thought. Perhaps he didn't suffer in death the way he had suffered in life.

"Can I go?" Tom Scott called.

"Do we have his information?" Gamache asked. Beauvoir nodded.

The chief rose. "You can go, but please don't leave the Inn and Spa."

"He gives me the creeps," said Dr. Harris, watching Scott disappear into the woods.

"Creeps?" asked Beauvoir. "Is that your medical judgment? Does he give you the willies, too?"

"No. You give me the willies."

"You wish." Beauvoir smiled and all but winked.

Dr. Harris blushed and silently cursed herself. Inspector Beauvoir was kneeling on the opposite side of the body. He was in his mid-thirties, lean, and athletic. His hair was dark and his eyes playful. Beauvoir always made her feel a little uncomfortable.

Chief Inspector Gamache was another matter. She found him very attractive, too, though not as a lover. In his mid-fifties, he was old enough to be her father. His dark hair was greying, and so was his trim moustache. Where Beauvoir was slim, Gamache was a large man, without being fat. Where Beauvoir was active, always moving, always ready with a quick comment, Gamache was calm. But the most striking thing about Armand Gamache was his deep brown eyes.

They were kind.

"Who is he?" Gamache looked at the man lying between them.

"That's why I called you over, Chief," said Beauvoir. "We don't know. We've been through his pockets, and there wasn't a wallet. Not even papers."

"Nothing? Not even a suicide note?"

Beauvoir shook his head. That was the real mystery. They'd find out who this man was easily enough, but the real question was, why didn't he write a note? Not everyone who committed suicide left a note, but not leaving one was rare. Most people wanted to explain. It was the last natural act of a person about to do something very unnatural.

"So far, nothing."

Gamache stood. The others joined him.

"What can you tell us, doctor?"

"I can tell you that he's in his late forties or early fifties. His hands are soft. He's an office worker, I'd say. His nails are trimmed. We didn't find anything under them."

"Nothing?" Gamache asked.

She shook her head.

"Are you sure?"

"Yes." Dr. Harris looked at Gamache. He rarely questioned her so closely. "Why?"

"I was just wondering."

"I'll have more for you later." She signalled the paramedics to take away the body and turned to follow them.

"May I join you?" Chief Inspector Gamache fell into step beside her. "Inspector Beauvoir will continue the work at the scene. I want to check the Inn and Spa."

"And the fact that the place is warm and you might find hot coffee there has nothing to do with it?"

"Nothing at all, doctor. I'm shocked at your suggestion." But he smiled a little as they followed the path out of the woods.

"Ever climb a tree, doctor?" he asked after a minute.

She grinned. "Of course I have. What Canadian child hasn't?"

"So have I," he said. "But that man hasn't. Not recently."

Chief Inspector Gamache nodded toward the body being carried just ahead of them.

"How do you know?" Dr. Harris asked.

"Think about it."

Under their feet, twigs snapped and dead maple leaves swished. The forest smelled of moss and pine.

Dr. Harris thought about climbing trees. Reaching for the branches. Worrying one would break and she'd fall. But that was part of the fun. Anything could happen.

And then she stopped, amazed that she'd missed it.

She looked down at her hands, then up into the chief's thoughtful eyes.

"His hands," she said. "They were clean. No dirt. No tree bark. He didn't climb that tree himself."

"No," said Gamache sadly. "He was helped up it and helped off it. He was murdered."

Chapter Three

Chief Inspector Gamache stood outside the Inn and Spa. It used to be a large private home, but it had been turned into a small hotel. The wide porch felt welcoming, and he could smell the smoke from a wood fire inside. The cold had chilled him, and he longed for warmth.

Pushing open the large wooden door, Gamache walked over to the front desk. A woman in her early forties looked up and smiled.

It was Dominique Gilbert, one of the owners of the Inn and Spa.

"Hello, Chief Inspector." She shook hands with the large man. "Come for a massage? Or perhaps a pedicure?"

"Sadly, no." He returned her smile. He liked Mrs. Gilbert. He'd met her on earlier cases in this part of Quebec. "I'm afraid my visit is much more serious in nature."

He watched as her smile faded and a look of worry crossed her face.

"What do you mean?"

"There's been a murder."

"Oh, no. Who?"

"I'm not sure. That's why I'm here. He might be one of your guests."

"Really? What's his name?"

"I don't know. I have a picture of him." The chief inspector studied Dominique Gilbert. She was a sensible woman. A former Montrealer who had moved to the country to open the Inn and Spa. It was a great success, but anything Dominique Gilbert did would likely succeed.

Dominique nodded, knowing what it meant to look at the picture. She steeled herself. "Of course. Angela?"

A woman in her mid-thirties appeared. "Yes, Mrs. Gilbert?"

"Could you look after the front desk?"

Dominique led the chief inspector into her office and closed the door. She squared her shoulders and looked directly at Gamache.

"I'm ready."

Armand Gamache thought she probably wasn't ready. No one could be prepared for what he was about to show her.

As she looked at the picture, her face became pained, as though he'd hit her.

"Are you all right?"

It was, he knew, a stupid question. Of course she wasn't all right. She'd just seen the face of a man strangled to death.

"I'm sorry," she kept saying, as if she had something to be sorry for.

Finally, colour returned to her face.

"What happened to him?"

Gamache chose to ignore her question. "Do you know him?"

"It's hard to say, but I think he might be Mr. Ellis. One of our guests."

"What can you tell me about Mr. Ellis?"

Chief Inspector Gamache led her to a comfortable chair. She sat and he pulled another chair over.

"Not much, I'm afraid, but Angela might be able to help. I think she checked him in."

He went to the door and quietly asked Angela to join them. There were no guests around, so she was able to leave the front desk.

"Is anything the matter?" she asked as she entered.

"Angela, this is Chief Inspector Gamache, of the Quebec Provincial Police. I'm afraid a man has been murdered, and he might have been one of our guests."

Angela's blue eyes widened. Red spread across her pale skin, moving up her neck to her cheeks.

A blusher, Gamache guessed. Some people were. They turned red when anyone so much as looked at them. Or was there another reason? Did this young woman know something?

"Angela," the chief inspector began, and Angela blushed to almost purple. "What can you tell me about Mr. Ellis?"

"Oh, no. It's not him, is it?"

"Please just answer the question." The chief made his demand gently.

"Well, he arrived two days ago. He was by himself. He'd booked a standard room, but since business is slow, I gave him a better one." Angela looked at Dominique for approval, and Dominique smiled at her. It occurred to Gamache that they were about the same age. But Angela seemed so young, and Dominique seemed, what? Not old. Mature.

"Is Mr. Ellis the dead man?" Angela asked.

"We think so," said Gamache. "Can you describe him?"

When she did, Gamache had little doubt that the man in the tree had been Mr. Ellis.

"You liked him?"

She nodded. "He seemed lonely. He always smiled, but his smile never reached his eyes, you know?"

Gamache did know. He'd met many people who could easily put a fake smile on their lips, but they could never put a fake sparkle into their eyes.

"Did he have any spa treatments?"

"None," said Angela.

"Was this his first visit?"

She nodded.

"Then why was he here?" Gamache asked.

.

"Not everyone comes for the spa, Chief Inspector," said Dominique, now fully recovered from her shock at seeing the dead man's picture. "Some are looking for peace and quiet."

Gamache thought of the dead man, swinging from the tree. He might have been looking for peace and quiet, but something else had found him. Something horrible.

Chapter Four

Chief Inspector Gamache stood alone in Mr. Ellis's room. Arthur, that was his first name on the register. He had paid cash and planned to be there a week. That was a long time to stay at a costly place. Dominique herself had been surprised when Angela had told her. Most guests were there two nights, maybe three. Few stayed longer.

Almost no one stayed a week.

And, as it turned out, Mr. Ellis didn't stay a week, either.

The chief inspector started a careful search of the room. It was very comfortable. And very tidy. Mr. Ellis had been an orderly man.

Gamache walked around, opening drawers and doors with his gloved hands. There were clothes neatly put away in the dresser and hung in the closet. Good clothes, but no designer labels.

Opening the medicine cabinet in the bathroom, he found nothing unusual. Though there was a bottle of extra-strong aspirin. Did Mr. Ellis get headaches? The bottle was half empty. In the Gamache home, a bottle of aspirin could last him and his wife a year or more. Gamache glanced at the "best before" date. Still two years away. It had to be a fairly new bottle, and yet it was already half gone.

He would ask Inspector Beauvoir to have the room searched for fingerprints, but he was certain this was where Mr. Ellis had spent his last days.

They had not found a wallet on the dead man, and there was no wallet here. No papers at all to say who he was. And yet Mr. Ellis had signed the register and told people his name. He did not seem to be hiding.

The facts didn't make sense. Soon, though, all the things that seemed so odd would begin to form a pattern. And in that pattern Chief Inspector Gamache would find a killer.

He stopped at the door for one last look.

Then he saw it: something white, leaning against the white pillow as though resting.

A letter.

Gamache picked up the envelope. It was unsealed. With his gloves still on, he removed a single sheet of lined paper with very neat writing on it. All the letters were carefully formed in black ink.

Did the writer know that the first person to read it would be a police officer?

Armand Gamache put on his half-moon reading glasses and walked to the window. There, in the sunshine, he read the dark words.

If you are reading this, my body has been found. I am sorry. I hope the discovery did not upset anyone. I tried to go as far away as possible so that no children would find me.

My work is finally done. I am tired, but I am at peace. Finally.

I know you cannot forgive me, but perhaps you can understand.

Gamache read the letter several times. It was a suicide note. He had read quite a few in his time, and none were clearer than this.

Lowering the letter, he took off his glasses. He sat in a chair and stared out the window at the horses in the field.

Mr. Ellis had intended to kill himself. And yet he had been murdered. Someone had beaten him to it.

Why?

Perhaps the murderer did not realize that Mr. Ellis was going to do the job himself. If the murderer had just waited a few hours, Ellis would have been dead by his own hand.

Unless.

Gamache looked at the letter again. It was neat, clear. Too clear? Surely someone about to end his life would tremble a bit? Would write quickly, before he changed his mind?

This note had been written by a steady hand. No emotion here. Not in the words. Not in the writing.

Once again, the chief looked out the window, as though the answer to his question was grazing in the field with the horses.

Then he smiled. But it was not a happy smile. It did not reach his thoughtful eyes.

He had his answer.

The letter he held had not been written by Mr. Ellis, but by his killer. The murderer had tried to make the death look as though Ellis had hanged himself. This letter was meant to confirm it.

Instead, the letter confirmed that Chief Inspector Gamache was on the trail of a cruel and cunning killer.

Chapter Five

Back downstairs in the entryway of the Inn and Spa, Gamache met Inspector Beauvoir.

"I've been thinking, Chief," said the inspector, taking off his hat. His hair, normally so neat, stood on end. "Not everyone could carry a dead man up a tree."

"Then tie a rope around his neck and throw him off," agreed Gamache.

"Exactly. I'm not sure I could."

"If you were afraid enough, you could," said the chief. He knew that fear was so powerful it made people do things they could not normally do. Like lift a car off a loved one. Or race into a burning building.

Fear saved lives.

But fear could also kill. It made men into murderers.

Beauvoir nodded. "Still, the killer would need to be young and strong."

From the entrance hall where they stood, they looked into the living room. Tom Scott was sitting by the fire. He had changed from his jogging clothes into jeans and a sweater. A workman was stacking wood for the fireplace, which was lit. Tom Scott ignored the man and put his feet up on the old coffee table.

Gamache handed his inspector the note he'd found and watched as Beauvoir's handsome face showed interest, then surprise.

"So what's the story?" Beauvoir asked. "Did he kill himself or not?"

"Not. I think that letter wasn't written by the dead man, but by his killer, to make the death look like suicide."

"Shit," said Beauvoir with a sigh. "Where did you find it?"

"In the dead man's room. His name is Ellis. First name is Arthur. I've locked the door." He handed the key to Beauvoir. "Can you get the scene-of-crime people to dust for fingerprints? And check the letter, too?"

At that moment Angela, the receptionist, appeared at Gamache's elbow. She smiled and waved into the living room.

"You know him?" Gamache nodded toward Tom Scott.

"Very well. He's my husband." She smiled.

"You're married to Tom Scott?" asked Inspector Beauvoir.

"No, of course not." Angela made a sour face and lowered her voice. "He's just strange. No, I mean him. Mike."

She pointed to the other man in the room. Mike was still filling the wood box.

"You both work here. That must be handy."

"It is," she agreed. Then her face became troubled. "Do you know what happened to poor Mr. Ellis?"

"Not yet, but we will. You liked Mr. Ellis," Gamache said, and she nodded. "More than other guests?"

"That is not a polite question," she said with a small smile.

"It was not meant to be polite." His eyes, still kind, hardened.

Angela's smile faded, and she seemed to make up her mind.

"You're right. He was nicer than some."

"Some in that room?" The chief glanced toward the living room and watched as Angela's eyes darted to Tom Scott.

"He tried to pick me up last night. Wanted to drive me home after work. I said no, but he was quite pushy. Finally, Mr. Ellis came over and told Mr. Scott to leave me alone."

"And how did Mr. Scott react?"

"He got angry, but when Mr. Ellis didn't back down, he said it was just a joke." Angela looked over at Tom Scott. "He's not very nice."

A bully, thought Gamache. He looked closely at Tom Scott, his dirty boots making marks on the nice table. Scott didn't care. Or perhaps he enjoyed making a mess, ruining things. He liked to hurt.

But did he like to kill?

Then Gamache remembered something. "Where was Mrs. Scott while all this was happening?"

"Mrs. Scott? I don't think he's married. Or if he is, she isn't here."

So, thought the chief, Scott lied about that. Why? It was a stupid lie, easily found out.

Stupid people worried Gamache. They were unpredictable.

"What did Mr. Ellis do yesterday?" he asked Angela.

"He spent the day in the village."

"In Three Pines?" Inspector Beauvoir asked. "Did he know anyone there?"

Angela paused to think. "I don't know. He asked a lot of questions about the village."

"What sort of questions?" Gamache wanted to know.

"Oh, whether Three Pines was a nice place to live. I had to tell him that my husband and I don't actually live there, but in St-Rémy, about twenty minutes away."

"He seems to have been very interested in you."

"Me?" She blushed. "No. He was just lonely, I think. Making conversation."

"Was he worried? Upset?" Beauvoir asked.

"No. He seemed calm. Most people arrive here stressed. They come to relax. He seemed pretty relaxed already." After a moment, she added, "Actually, that isn't the right word. He wasn't relaxed, he was tired, as if he had no energy left."

Gamache watched the scene-of-crime team go up to Ellis's room. Why did Ellis choose to come here, anyway? he asked himself.

While the team searched Ellis's room and car, Chief Inspector Gamache walked down the dirt road into the tiny village.

Three Pines sat quietly in a valley, as though hiding from the world. And the world certainly seemed fooled.

Old homes faced the village green, a round and very pretty park. Wood smoke rose from chimneys, and the fresh, clean air smelled a bit of maple logs.

Three Pines was at peace.

That reminded the chief inspector of the note he'd recently read. And of the man found hanging, like a late fall leaf, from a tree.

"*I am tired,*" Gamache murmured as he walked into the gentle little village. "*But I am at peace.*"

Chapter Six

Chief Inspector Gamache warmed himself by the fire in the bistro. Around him, other customers drank hot chocolate and coffee and ate pastries. Fires roared in the fireplaces at both ends of the cozy room. Gamache took a sip of coffee and ate a pastry. The November cold had gotten into his bones even on the short walk, and he was only now warming up. He spared a moment to think of Inspector Beauvoir and the rest of the team, now on their hands and knees searching for clues at the Inn and Spa. Then he took a bite of the cream-filled pastry and turned his attention to the large man across from him.

Gabri was one of the owners of both this bistro and the Bed and Breakfast across the village green. He was big, some might even say fat, though they would only say so if he couldn't hear them. Gabri was a happy man, content with his quiet life in the quiet village.

Around Gamache and Gabri, people were laughing and talking. Light danced off the shiny wood floors, and Gamache sank deeper into the large, comfortable armchair. Gabri sat on a faded sofa across from him and sipped tea.

"It's great to see you again, Chief Inspector," said Gabri. "Just visiting?"

"I wish. I'm afraid there's been a death."

Gabri turned pale. "Here in Three Pines?"

"In the forest. A man was found hanged."

Gabri sighed and shook his head. "Who was he? Someone we know?"

"He was a guest at the Inn and Spa. His name was Ellis."

"First or last name?"

"Last. His first name was Arthur."

Gabri thought, then shook his head again.

Gamache brought out the photograph. He hated showing it. Making people look at the dead man's face seemed like an assault. But he had no choice.

Gabri looked quickly at the picture. "I know him." He turned back to Gamache. "Didn't catch his name, though. He came in here yesterday. Myrna!"

A large black woman in a long, loose orange dress ambled over. She smiled when she saw the chief inspector. But her smile faded when she saw their serious faces.

The chief inspector rose and bowed slightly.

"Hello," she said. "Here on business?"

Gabri patted the seat next to him on the sofa, and she sat.

"Has someone died?" She looked from Gamache to her friend Gabri.

"A man was found hanging in the woods. That guy who came in yesterday. He had lunch here, then visited your store," said Gabri.

Myrna owned a bookstore next to the bistro. Her shop was a gathering place for villagers. They'd find a book, sit by her wood stove, enjoy a cup of strong tea, and read. She didn't care if they actually bought the book. She just liked the company. And so did her customers.

"The tall man? Quiet?" Myrna asked, and Gabri nodded.

"Was he looking for a special book?" Chief Inspector Gamache asked.

"As far as I know, he wasn't looking for a book at all. He wanted to know about the village and the area."

"Just making conversation?" Gamache asked.

"I thought so."

"But now?"

"Now that I think about it, he seemed interested in whether this was a good place for young men to put down roots. His question seemed odd, since he wasn't a young man," said Myrna.

"Funny," Gabri jumped in. "He asked me the same question. Wanted to know if there were many young men around. Aside from me, though, I couldn't think of any."

Both Gamache and Myrna looked at Gabri. He was many things, but young wasn't one of them.

"It must be nice to live in your head, my dear." Myrna smiled.

"It is, you know," agreed Gabri. "In my head I'm young and slim and very rich."

"You are, for sure," said Chief Inspector Gamache. He knew that Gabri and Myrna were very rich indeed, rich in the things that matter. In friendships and laughter, in kindness and company.

People rich in money might belong at the Inn and Spa, but those rich in other ways belonged in the tiny village of Three Pines. Here, kindness was the real currency.

"But there are a lot of young men around," said Gamache, accepting a refill of coffee from the waiter, who was a young man.

"True, but I think he was asking about people moving here, not born here," said Gabri.

"I thought the same thing," said Myrna. "I asked if he had anyone in mind, his son, maybe."

"What did he say?"

"It was strange. He seemed to be about to say something, but then he shook his head and left."

Gamache turned to Gabri. "Do you have anyone staying at the Bed and Breakfast?"

"Yes, as a matter of fact. A woman arrived a couple of days ago, and then last night a fellow showed up."

"With reservations?"

"Well, the woman called ahead but the man just arrived. Took a room for a couple of days."

"Did you tell Mr. Ellis about him?" Gamache asked.

"Well, no. He hadn't shown up yet."

"Poor man," said Myrna at last. "Killing himself."

"Can't say I blame him," said Gabri, looking out the window at the dreary, cold day. "Depressing weather, and worse to come."

"The odd thing is, most suicides don't happen in the fall or even in the winter," said Myrna. "They happen in April, just as the weather is getting better."

"Really?" Gabri turned to her, surprised. Gamache was not surprised. He knew that what she said was true.

"People rarely take their lives when things are at their worst," said Myrna. "The sad fact is that they kill themselves when things are beginning to look better."

"But that doesn't make sense," said Gabri, who could not imagine killing anyone as wonderful as himself.

"When people are really depressed, they don't have the energy to kill themselves," said Myrna, who had once been a therapist in Montreal. "But as soon as they start feeling a little better, their energy comes back. They're still depressed, but now they can act."

"How sad he must have been," said Gabri.

"It's not sadness that drives most people to take their lives," said Myrna. "It's emptiness. Loneliness."

Chief Inspector Gamache leaned forward. "But Mr. Ellis didn't kill himself. He was murdered."

Two very surprised people looked back at him.

"Someone hanged him from a tree?" Myrna asked.

"I'm afraid so. They tried to make his death look like suicide. Even wrote a note. But it was murder."

"How horrible," said Gabri.

"His name was Ellis?" Myrna asked.

"Mean anything to you?" Gamache asked. "Is there an Ellis family nearby?"

Both Myrna and Gabri shook their heads. Myrna got up.

"If there's anything I can do to help, let me know." She walked away.

"Arthur Ellis," said Gabri, almost to himself. "He sounds so normal. Seemed so normal."

Gamache had to agree. But he also knew normal people were killed all the time. It was the murderer who wasn't normal.

Unseen by either man, Myrna paused in the doorway of her bookstore.

She stared back at the two men, puzzled.

Chapter Seven

――――

"Chief? It's Beauvoir."

Gamache stood at the bar of the bistro, holding the phone to his ear. Cell phones did not work in Three Pines. So Inspector Beauvoir had had to call the bistro to speak to his boss.

"Find anything?" Gamache asked.

"Not much," said Beauvoir. "We searched Ellis's room and took fingerprints. His car is in the lot. Ontario plates. The Ontario police are finding out who owns the car. Should know more soon. But I did find something interesting. That note you found in Ellis's room?"

"Yes?"

"It was written by Ellis himself. Not the murderer. In fact, I'm not so sure there is a murderer."

"How do you know Mr. Ellis wrote it?" asked Gamache, surprised.

"The writing matches his writing in the registration book at the Inn."

Gamache took a long, deep breath and exhaled. This was unexpected. Was it possible that Arthur Ellis had killed himself after all?

The chief inspector closed his eyes and the cheerful bistro disappeared. Now he saw the gently swinging body in the cold, dead forest. And the clean hands. Could he have been wrong? Had Ellis climbed up the tree himself? Maybe he wiped his hands on his pants and got the dirt off.

Certainly, everything he was hearing about Mr. Ellis pointed to a lonely man who might have taken his own life.

But why come into the village and ask about young men?

No, there were questions still.

"Can you read the note to me again?"

"*If you are reading this, my body has been found,*" Beauvoir read over the phone. "*I am sorry. I hope the discovery did not upset anyone. I tried to go as far away as possible so that no children would find me. My work is finally done.*

I am tired, but I am at peace. Finally. I know you cannot forgive me, but perhaps you can understand."

There was silence as both men thought about what the note said.

"It's a suicide note," said the chief at last. There was no doubt. Beauvoir was right. Should he be happy, though? Relieved that this poor man at least hadn't suffered the terror of being murdered?

No. There was nothing to be happy about here. Mr. Ellis had clearly suffered other things in his life. Suffered enough that he could no longer stand the pain.

I am tired, but I am at peace. Finally.

But there was something else he had written.

"Can you read it to me again, please?"

Gamache listened to the now-familiar words. "What did he mean by *My work is finally done*?"

"Maybe his kids were grown up, or he'd retired. I guess we'll find out soon enough."

"But the note wasn't addressed to anyone, was it? Not to children or a wife. No one," said Gamache.

"True. But that isn't unusual."

"And the note isn't signed. That's more unusual," said Gamache.

"What are you getting at, chief?"

"I'm just wondering," said Gamache. At that moment, a shadow fell across the bar where he stood talking on the bistro telephone. Looking up, he saw Myrna beside him. She had a book in her hand and a very serious look on her face.

"Can you call Dr. Harris and see if she has any autopsy results?" Gamache asked Inspector Beauvoir before hanging up and greeting Myrna. Once again he bowed slightly, and waved toward a nearby table.

"You look like you could use a drink," he said as they sat. It was now past noon. The bistro was filling with lunch customers and the smell of fresh bread and garlic and hearty stews.

"You'll need one, too, once you see this."

Gamache ordered Myrna a beer and looked at the book she had placed on the wooden table between them. It had a hard cover. Gamache picked it up and scanned it, as Myrna sipped her beer. It was a murder mystery by a Canadian writer. Barbara Fradkin. It looked very good, and Gamache thought he might buy it, but he wondered why Myrna had come back to the bistro just for this.

He lowered the book and looked at her.

She took it back, turned it over, and placed one very large finger on a large sentence on the back cover.

"Winner of the Arthur Ellis Award for Best Mystery in Canada."

Gamache's eyes widened, and he looked at Myrna, who was smiling slightly.

"I knew the name was familiar," she said. "You kept calling him Mr. Ellis, but the name didn't click until I was leaving and heard Gabri say 'Arthur Ellis.'" I went through my books, and there I found it. Arthur Ellis. It's an award. For murder mysteries."

"Is it a coincidence?" Gamache asked.

"You tell me."

Gamache stared at the book. As the head of homicide for the Quebec Provincial Police, he'd come to realize that coincidences almost never happened in murder cases.

"Was Arthur Ellis a mystery writer, too? Is that why the award is named for him?"

"No. This is where things gets strange."

"Stranger than they already are?" he asked.

"Lots," said Myrna. "Arthur Ellis was the name of Canada's official executioner. He hanged people."

Chapter Eight

Fifteen minutes later, Inspector Beauvoir joined Gamache in the bookstore. As soon as Beauvoir walked through the door, Gamache handed him the book. The chief had on his half-moon reading glasses and looked at the inspector over them.

Beauvoir took the book, and Gamache went back to the computer screen on Myrna's desk. Myrna herself was reading over the chief's shoulder.

Inspector Beauvoir looked at the murder mystery in his hand. He was confused.

"Was it a copycat murder? Is the answer in here?" He held up the book. "Did this Barbara Fradkin kill Mr. Ellis?"

Once again, Gamache looked up, this time with a small smile. "I don't think so, but that book certainly holds a clue. With Myrna's help, I've found Arthur Ellis."

Gamache got up and offered his seat to his second-in-command. Beauvoir sat and looked at the computer screen. On it was a black-and-white photo of a middle-aged man. It was taken in 1912. He had on round glasses, an old-fashioned hat, and a suit. He looked like a banker.

But he wasn't.

He was Arthur Ellis.

As Inspector Beauvoir read, his breathing all ...ped. Finally, he sat back from the screen. ...d up at Chief Inspector Gamache and ...yrna.

"What does it mean?" he asked, almost to himself. "It can't be the same Arthur Ellis."

That would make the man 150 years old. A zombie. A vampire. But not immortal.

For Arthur Ellis had just died. Hanged in the woods.

"It means," said Gamache, leading the inspector into the bistro, "that we have a mystery on our hands."

"No shit," said Beauvoir.

Over a lunch of steak and fries, the two men discussed what they had found.

"So, Arthur Ellis killed people," said Beauvoir, popping a salted fry into his mouth.

"He executed them," Gamache corrected. "There is a fine line between the two. He was Canada's official hangman."

Beauvoir shook his head, remembering the photo of the mild-looking man. Had he really killed, executed, hundreds of men and women in the early 1900s? Hired by the Canadian government to hang them?

"Hell of a job." Beauvoir wondered how that went down at dinner parties. Or on first dates.

"He came from a long line of executioners," said the chief, taking a sip of beer. "Learned it from his father in England. His family had been hanging people for three hundred years."

"Lucky us, to get him," said Beauvoir.

"Arthur Ellis wasn't his real name," said Gamache. "He wanted to hide who he really was. He knew people hated and feared the executioner. They wanted someone to do the job, but they didn't want to know that person."

Beauvoir nodded. He'd read the story on the Web, just as the chief inspector had. He knew the rest. That after a long, successful career, Arthur Ellis had made a mistake.

A terrible mistake.

He was to hang a woman in Montreal, in 1935. But he got her weight wrong, and instead of breaking her neck, the drop took her head off.

It was his last execution. He couldn't do the job anymore. He died three years later in Montreal. A broken, lonely man.

The waiter took away their empty plates.

Beauvoir leaned forward. "How is it that Arthur Ellis was found hanging in the woods outside Three Pines this morning?"

That was the question.

The chief inspector put down his mug of beer. "I don't know. The official hangman chose Arthur Ellis as an alias a hundred years ago. I think our dead man chose the same alias. He chose Arthur Ellis for a reason."

Beauvoir looked into the deep, thoughtful eyes of his boss. And he knew Gamache was right.

"He was here to execute someone?" Beauvoir asked.

Gamache stood up, paid, and made for the door.

"I think so."

They walked across the bridge to the old railway station, where Gamache's team had set up an office. Phones were ringing, and urgent messages awaited both men.

Ten minutes later, Beauvoir pulled a chair up to the chief inspector's desk. Gamache removed his reading glasses, finished his phone call, and looked at his inspector.

"Dr. Harris found bruises under the rope marks on the body," said Gamache. "The man was strangled, probably by a belt. Then he was hanged. She's confirmed it. Our man was murdered."

"And I know who he was," said Beauvoir. "His name was James Hill. Ontario's motor vehicles branch confirmed it. We traced his licence plate."

"Good. We're getting there."

For the rest of the afternoon, Inspector Beauvoir tracked down all the information he could on James Hill. Where he worked, lived. His family. His friends.

Chief Inspector Gamache went on his own hunt.

Myrna and Gabri had both said this James Hill had asked about young men in Three Pines. And a young man had appeared at the Bed and Breakfast the night before. Unexpectedly. At about the same time that James Hill was killed.

As the chief inspector crossed the village green, he could see geese in graceful formation overhead, flying south for the winter. But Gamache's mind was elsewhere. On something not nearly so natural.

Who was James Hill here to execute? And who had got to him first?

Chapter Nine

——

Paul Goulet turned out to be a nice young man. He had a ready smile and warm eyes.

"How can I help you, Chief Inspector?"

They stood on the wide porch of the Bed and Breakfast. Paul was in his bicycling outfit of very tight pants and a very tight top. Armand Gamache was glad those clothes didn't exist when he was twenty years old. And he vowed never to wear them now. Not that his wife Reine-Marie would allow it. The two of them often went for slow, quiet bike rides around the mountain in Montreal, sometimes taking a picnic.

But when Gamache saw what Goulet was wearing, he suddenly knew why bicyclists went so fast these days. He would, too, if he were wearing basically nothing.

"It's a pretty village, isn't it," said Paul. "What's it called again?"

"Three Pines."

"Because of them?" He pointed to the three tall pine trees at the far end of the village green.

"Yes. It's an old code. Three pine trees planted together means safety. It was used as a signal centuries ago. It marked a sanctuary."

Paul Goulet was silent, and Gamache turned to look at him. If the chief inspector had not been standing so close, he would never have noticed the two warm lines that appeared on the young man's cheeks.

Gamache waited until the tears stopped.

"Why does that idea move you so much?" the chief asked.

"Who doesn't long for safety?"

"The man who already has it. Are you looking for safety?"

"I don't know. I didn't think so, until you told me that story."

"Why are you here?" Gamache asked quietly.

"I took a week off to bike around. No plans, just a map of the bike paths. I arrived last night and found this place."

He seemed almost in awe at the pretty, gentle village.

"You're with the police, you say?" he looked at Gamache. "Has something happened?"

"There's been a death." Gamache watched Paul for a reaction. He seemed polite, interested. But nothing more.

"I'm sorry. Someone from here?"

"No, a visitor. Like you. A man named James Hill."

Still Paul Goulet looked blank. Chief Inspector Gamache knew how difficult that was. A person's face almost always had some expression on it.

A blank face was a wall. Put there on purpose, to hide something.

"Where are you from?" Gamache asked.

"Ottawa. I go to school there."

"What are you taking?"

"A general degree. Haven't decided on a career yet."

Paul Goulet smiled. It was an easy grin. Gamache hoped this young man was not involved in the death, but he was far from sure.

Strong young arms and legs had lifted Hill's body into the tree, tied a rope around his neck, and thrown him off.

Paul's tight suit made it clear that he had strong arms and legs.

"The dead man was going under another name," Gamache said. "Arthur Ellis."

"Why would he do that?"

"We don't know. But someone murdered him."

"You mean there's a killer in this village?"

"There's a killer in every village. In every home. In every heart," said Gamache, watching Paul closely. "All anyone needs is the right reason."

The young man stared back but didn't say anything. Finally he got up.

"If I can help, I will," he said. "But I can't see how. Can I go for my bike ride?"

Gamache nodded. "But don't go far."

Paul climbed onto his bike and with a shove was off down the dirt road.

After that, Chief Inspector Gamache found the woman who was also staying at the Bed and Breakfast. Her name was Sue Gravel. She was thirty-eight and worked as a secretary in a law firm in Montreal. She'd arrived a few days earlier and was planning to leave the next day.

No, she knew no one in Three Pines. It struck her as a boring place. Nothing to do.

"Then why did you come here?" Gamache asked.

"To relax."

Gamache smiled. Only an amazing person could really relax. Sue Gravel did not strike the chief inspector as an amazing person.

She complained all the way through the interview. The weather was cold and damp. No shopping. No high-speed internet. And her cell phone didn't work.

How could you relax here? she demanded.

Gamache did not suggest that she go for a walk or buy a book and sit by the fire in the bistro. He did not suggest that she sit quietly and get to know herself so she could be all the company she needed.

Had this woman killed James Hill? Murder would at least have been something to do. But while he liked the idea of arresting her, Gamache resisted.

He spent the rest of the afternoon interviewing the waiters at the bistro, the clerk at the general store, the young helper at the pastry shop. Then he climbed the slope to the Inn and Spa.

James Hill had chosen to spend his last days on earth here. Had his killer, too?

Chapter Ten

There were no young men among the guests at the Inn and Spa. The average age seemed to be ninety-seven. Except Tom Scott. The man who'd found the body. The man who'd lied about having a wife.

Chief Inspector Gamache sat across from him. Tom picked at a thread coming loose from his sweater.

"Why did you lie about having a wife?"

"Oh, that. I was joking."

Gamache leaned forward and lowered his voice. "You were not joking." Each word was said slowly, clearly.

"There is no wife," admitted Tom Scott. The words hurried from him, like hostages trapped for years. "I made her up. Sometimes I give her a name. Kathy. We go to parties and movies and take long walks together. And we visit friends in the country."

There was a long, long silence then. Armand Gamache sat still, waiting. The fire in the grate mumbled and popped. Tom Scott had closed his eyes. Gamache knew what he was doing. What all liars did.

He was looking for a way out. A back door. Another lie. A way to make this better.

The silence stretched on. Armand Gamache waited.

"I'm so lonely," Scott finally whispered. "No one knows. It used to be an ache, a physical pain. Now even that's gone. And there's nothing. Nothing. I even tried to pick up that receptionist woman. I didn't want to do anything. Just talk. I offered her a lift home, but she refused. I was trying to help, and she looked at me like I was crap."

He sighed and opened his eyes.

"I couldn't stand it anymore. I'm thirty-eight years old. Not even halfway through my life. I couldn't see living like this for another month, never mind forty years."

"What was your plan?" Gamache asked, though he suspected the answer. It was the April plan.

"I wasn't sure. I wanted to come to a fancy place. Have the best room, eat the best food. See if I'd be happy then. But it didn't work. I went for a walk in the woods, trying to think of what to do. I don't want to live, but I'm too afraid to die."

"Is that when you found the dead man?"

"Yes." He looked into Gamache's eyes. This time with wonder. "Do you think it was a sign from God?"

"Saying what?"

"That I shouldn't kill myself. That this is what it looks like. It looked horrible."

"You think God would kill a man to save you?" Gamache asked. His voice wasn't accusing. It was curious. The ways of the Creator, he knew, were hard to fathom. But not nearly as hard as the ways of the created.

"I think maybe the man was going to kill himself anyway, and maybe the gift was having me find him."

Gamache smiled then. Sometimes hope takes its time, but it finally appears. If you hold on just long enough. And he saw it now, deep down in Tom Scott's eyes. A tiny spring.

But that did not mean that Tom Scott wasn't a killer. A man willing to die could also be willing to kill.

"Did Arthur Ellis ever speak to you?" Gamache asked.

Scott hesitated. "He saw me talking to that receptionist…"

"Angela."

"Yes, her, and he asked me to stop. We had words."

"Angry words?"

Scott nodded.

"Anything else?" Gamache asked.

"Before that, we'd talked a little. He wanted to know where I was from."

"What did you tell him?"

"I said I was a New Yorker. An investment banker." Scott managed a weak smile and shrugged. Old habits.

"Did he believe you?"

"I don't think he cared. Most people don't."

But Gamache disagreed. He suspected Arthur Ellis, or James Hill, cared deeply.

Gamache went in search of Angela and found her talking to her husband. He was of medium height and heavy-set. His hair was thick and a brilliant red.

"Hello." Gamache smiled.

"Chief Inspector, this is my husband, Mike." They shook hands.

"Did Mr. Ellis speak to you?" he asked Mike.

"No. He thanked me for opening a door for him once. He seemed polite but quiet. Like he didn't want company."

Gamache turned to Angela. "But he spoke to you quite a bit, it seems."

As usual, she blushed. "Well, I guess I was the one who kept talking to him. He just seemed so alone."

"Did he tell you anything about himself?"

"Only that he was here for a vacation and that he had a son who would love to live in a place like this. He wondered if there were many jobs for young people."

"Chief Inspector?" Dominique Gilbert popped her head through the living room door. "There's a phone call for you."

"Chief," came Beauvoir's voice. "I know why James Hill was here."

Chapter Eleven

Chief Inspector Gamache met Beauvoir at the bench on the village green. Around them, villagers walked dogs. They did their shopping. Some worked in their gardens. But no one stopped moving. It was too cold.

But the two men on the bench had something worse than cold to worry about. They had murder on their minds.

Gamache pulled his coat tighter around him and looked at his inspector.

"Okay," said Beauvoir. "We ran James Hill's fingerprints and licence plate. He lived and worked in Ottawa. With the government. In the Department of Records."

Armand Gamache shifted a bit on the bench. The Department of Records. It was huge, of course. It kept track of Canada's official documents. Not people's private lives, but their public ones. Taxes, passports, court papers. Any time a Canadian came in contact with the government, the records ended up in James Hill's department.

"He took the job fifteen years ago. Before that, he was living in Thunder Bay."

"In northwestern Ontario?"

"Exactly. With his wife and daughter. But they were killed twenty years ago. Their car was hit by a pickup truck filled with kids."

Gamache looked down briefly. He could not imagine surviving the loss of his own wife and daughter. How had James Hill coped?

"Here's a picture of them."

From a file folder Beauvoir pulled a printout of a newspaper article. It showed a young James Hill, smiling. His pretty wife, also beaming. And their daughter. Debbie. She looked like her mother. Dark hair, laughing.

Gone, in a moment.

Gamache felt an almost physical pain. A terrible loss.

He scanned the article.

Mrs. Hill and Debbie had been returning from a birthday party when their car was side-swiped. They slid off the road, down a cliff. Both died at the scene.

The other vehicle had four kids in it. Two boys. Two girls. Three were sixteen years old. One was fifteen. None seriously injured.

The chief inspector looked at Beauvoir.

"What happened?"

"The cops investigated, of course. It was clear that the kids had hit the Hill car. What wasn't clear was who was driving."

Gamache nodded. He could see that coming.

"By the time help arrived, the kids had gotten out of the truck. They had minor injuries, but that was all. One of them had wiped the steering wheel. To get the blood off, he said, but everyone suspected that he did it to protect whoever was driving."

"Fingerprints," said Gamache. "No convictions?"

"Not even an arrest. Hill spent years trying to get someone to take the blame. But the kids' lawyers wouldn't even let them say they were sorry. They just stopped talking."

Gamache was silent for a moment, thinking.

"So finally James Hill moved away," said the chief. "To Ottawa."

"To the Department of Records," said Beauvoir. He held up another file. "Hill was a busy man."

Beauvoir handed the file to Gamache. In it were more reports, of more deaths. A young man killed ten years ago in Victoria. A young woman killed seven years ago in Halifax.

Both hanged.

"Arthur Ellis," said Gamache. Beauvoir nodded.

The official executioner, alive again. And passing death sentences.

"The victims were two of the people in the truck that night," said Beauvoir.

"Both murdered," said Gamache. "One on the west coast, the other on the east. No police force would connect the two."

"Exactly," said Beauvoir. "In fact, the first was considered a suicide, but the cause of death was changed to murder later. No one was arrested."

"James Hill," said Gamache. He got up from the bench and started walking slowly around the edge of the village green. Beauvoir joined him and listened as the chief thought out loud. "He got his job so he could find the four young people in the pickup. And when he found them, he killed them."

"Didn't just kill," said Beauvoir. "He executed them. Sentenced them to death."

Gamache thought of the young men and women in the truck that night. How horrible it must have been for them. Did the guilt weigh them down? Or were they so scared they hid it away? Comforted themselves with the lie that the accident wasn't their fault.

But Gamache knew what happened when a terrible truth was buried. It didn't just go to sleep. No. It grew. Big. It became huge. Monstrous. It ate away a person's insides.

And left him hollow. Empty.

That's what had happened to those four kids. That's what had happened to James Hill, too. He'd died in the car that night, with his wife and daughter. Hill had died in spirit and Arthur Ellis had been reborn in him. Now he had one goal. To punish the young men and women who had killed his wife and daughter.

Chief Inspector Gamache put his hands behind his back and thought as he walked.

"James Hill used his position at the Department of Records to track down two of the people in the truck, and he killed them," Gamache said. "What about the other two?"

"I think one of them is here," said Beauvoir. "He tracked him here and intended to hang him."

"That's why he was asking about young men?" Gamache asked.

"Yes. But that doesn't make sense," said Beauvoir. "If the kids were sixteen when this happened, they'd be almost forty now. Not exactly young."

"True. When was the last time you visited your mother?"

"Oh, Jesus, she hasn't gotten to you, too?"

Gamache smiled. "No. I'm just wondering."

"A couple of weeks ago. We went over for dinner. Why?"

"What did she make?"

"My favourite. What she always makes when I visit. Beef stew."

"She's made it for you since you were a kid, right?"

"Right. Why are we talking about my mother?"

"When our children come home, we do the same thing. Make their favourite foods. Annie had to explain the other day that pink cupcakes aren't actually her favourite anymore. We knew that, but still we make them."

"Is this going anywhere, or have you finally lost your mind? Sir."

Gamache laughed. "Perhaps a bit of both. My point is that parents always see their children as children. In our heads, we know their real age, but in our hearts, they're still kids. I think that's what happened with Hill."

"He sees his daughter as a child?" asked Beauvoir, a little lost.

"Probably. But I meant the kids in the pickup. The last time he saw them, they were in their teens. Their images must have been burned into his mind. He would forever see them as teens."

"He talked about a young man," said Beauvoir, "but he was actually looking for someone much older."

"In his mid- to late thirties," said Gamache. "Who are the two survivors from that truck?"

"Cindy Pane and Tim Short."

"Tim Short," said Gamache. "Tom Scott?"

He stopped walking and looked into the distance. "And yet, perhaps he was lying," the chief murmured. "Covering up."

"What did you say?" asked Beauvoir.

Gamache turned to look at him. "James Hill came here to kill someone. Execute, he would say. But it comes to the same thing. He would hang his victim from a tree. But was it a *him* he was looking for? Or a *her*?"

"He said 'him.' He said 'young man.'"

"True," said Gamache, walking again. "But he also said his name was Arthur Ellis. He lied once, maybe he lied twice."

They walked quickly up the slope, headed to the Inn and Spa.

"You think he wasn't looking for a man," said Beauvoir. "He was looking for a woman."

Chapter Twelve

Chief Inspector Gamache looked around the group at the Inn and Spa. They were all in the living room. A fire crackled in the grate, tended by Mike, the handyman. His wife, Angela, the receptionist, was there. Dominique, the owner, stood by the grand piano. She looked nervous. She'd put out tea and a plate of cookies. But she suspected that this was not a social event.

Sue Gravel, from the Bed and Breakfast, sat in the best chair. The large one by the fire. She looked sour and hugged herself, but Gamache knew the chill she felt came from within.

"Nice place," said young Paul Goulet. He had returned from his bicycle ride just in time to change and join them.

They all looked at Chief Inspector Gamache, who stood by the fireplace. Waiting.

Finally the last member of the group arrived.

Tom Scott looked surprised to see so many people. He paused, then sat in a chair by the door. Outside of the circle made by the other people.

"Why are we here?" Dominique asked.

She was polite but puzzled.

"We're here to catch a killer," said Gamache. He looked at each of them. Some were afraid. Some were annoyed. Some were amused.

And one was a murderer.

"Last night, one of your guests was killed," he said to Dominique. "He'd arrived the day before and signed himself in as Arthur Ellis. He spent the day in Three Pines, asking questions. He seemed most interested in young men of the area. But Arthur Ellis had a secret. And like most people with secrets, he told a lot of lies."

Gamache looked beyond the circle of chairs. To the one on the outside. To Tom Scott.

"This morning, while supposedly jogging, you found his body hanging from a tree. You called for help. But then you did something very curious. Actually, you didn't do something. You didn't try to get him down."

"He was obviously dead," snapped Tom.

"And yet most people would try," said the chief. "It would be a natural reaction. Unless you already knew he was dead. And had been for some time."

Gamache turned back to the room.

"Like most murders, this one was about secrets and lies. But hidden below all those lies was an emotion. Sorrow. A sorrow so great it turned into a monster. And that monster finally consumed the man."

The chief paused. All eyes were on him. The only sound was the mumbling of the fire.

"And that is when Arthur Ellis was born. Or, rather, reborn."

The people in the room looked at each other.

"What do you mean?" asked Angela.

"Arthur Ellis was not his real name. His real name was James Hill."

Gamache watched them. Paul shifted in his seat. Angela blushed, of course. Mike poked the fire. Sue? She dropped her eyes and clutched herself even tighter.

"James Hill had lost his wife and child in an accident twenty years ago, when they were hit by a truck. No one was arrested. There was no trial or even an apology. No one was held responsible. And yet his wife and child were dead."

Now they looked at each other, eyes darting from face to face.

"An injustice had been done," said Gamache. "And James Hill, full of rage, came up with a plan. He would track down each and every person in that truck, and he would kill them."

Gamache picked up the file from the table in front of him.

"Over the years, he tracked down two of them. They were found hanged."

"Psycho," said Tom Scott.

"But why did he change his name to Arthur Ellis?" Dominique asked.

"Arthur Ellis was the alias of Canada's official hangman," said the chief inspector. "James Hill used the same alias when he was on the trail of his next victim."

"Oh, God," said Angela. Mike sat and put his arms around her.

"There is a murderer in this room. A person who has been involved in at least three deaths. The young Hill family, twenty years ago, and now the murder of the father. James Hill."

"But you say he came here to kill someone," said Paul. "Who?"

"That's the question," agreed Gamache. "Who had James Hill found in Three Pines? Which of the young people from the pickup? One man and one woman were left. Which of them was it?"

"Mr. Ellis was asking about young men," said Angela. "Was that why? But that doesn't make sense. He wouldn't be young anymore."

"Ellis lied," said Gamache. "There has been a lot of lying in this case."

His gaze came to rest on Tom Scott.

"He lied about his name," the chief continued. "He lied about why he was here. Could he also have been lying about looking for a man? Maybe it was a woman. Maybe he wanted to put his victim at ease. Throw her off."

Gamache turned to Sue Gravel.

"Maybe he was looking for a woman. Or"
— now he shifted his gaze to Paul Goulet —
"maybe he was telling the truth. Maybe one of
the people in the truck twenty years ago had
had a child of his own. And maybe James Hill
wanted to hurt him the way he'd been hurt. By
killing, not the man himself, but his child."

Paul Goulet stood up. Across the room,
Inspector Beauvoir tensed. Ready to tackle Goulet
if he threatened the chief. But Goulet simply
stared, his eyes narrow and cold.

"So what are you saying, Chief Inspector?"
Dominique asked. "That he could have been
looking for a man or a woman or a young person
or an older person? Doesn't exactly narrow it
down."

"No," admitted Gamache. "But this does."

From the file he took a slim piece of paper
and read.

*If you are reading this, my body has been
found. I am sorry. I hope the discovery
did not upset anyone. I tried to go as far
away as possible so that no children would
find me.*

My work is finally done. I am tired, but I am at peace. Finally.

I know you cannot forgive me, but perhaps you can understand.

"I wondered why it wasn't addressed to anyone. Some suicide letters aren't signed. But most are at least addressed to someone. This man had no one to write to. No family. But he did want people to know that it was over. And that's the key."

Gamache put the note on the coffee table, next to the cookies.

"*My work is finally done,*" he quoted. "What did he mean by that?"

"That he'd killed the last person from that truck, obviously," said Paul.

"Exactly." Gamache turned to him.

There was silence in the room. Every eye was on the chief inspector.

"I am arresting you for the murder of James Hill," he said. He stepped forward, as did Inspector Beauvoir. Just in time to catch Angela and Mike as they tried to flee.

Chapter Thirteen

Armand Gamache swirled the scotch in his glass. Around the table sat Dominique, Myrna, and Gabri.

"How did you know?" Dominique asked.

"It was really the only answer. They were the right age..."

"But a lot of people were the right age," Myrna interrupted.

"True. But there was something else," said Gamache. "His work was done. He planned to kill himself. He had no reason to live."

They thought about that while Gamache waited. Finally, Gabri lowered his beer and smiled, but without humour. His sad smile did not reach his eyes.

"His work was done because he had found, not one, but two," said Gabri. "He'd found the last two kids from the pickup."

Gamache nodded.

"Angela and Mike had moved away and married. When they learned what had happened to their two friends, they realized that the killer would be after them. So they changed their names and moved here. Working for cash, so there'd be less of a trail."

"How did James Hill find them?" Myrna asked, taking a fistful of nuts.

"His job at the Department of Records. He knew they'd married. But there were no records after that. They disappeared. Then Mike made a mistake. He applied for a social insurance number using his old name. He needed it to get the money left to him in his parents' will."

"The SIN number," said Dominique. "Ironic."

"James Hill knew Mike was somewhere in the area," said Gamache. "But he didn't know where. He booked into the Inn and Spa and started looking."

"Not realizing that Mike was right there," said Dominique. "Didn't he recognize him?"

"Would you?" asked Gabri. "A guy changes a lot from sixteen to thirty-six. Except me, of course."

"Of course," said Myrna, rolling her eyes.

"James Hill did not recognize either of them," said Gamache. "But they recognized him immediately. He'd been in his late twenties when the accident happened. He'd have aged, but not changed all that much. They realized Hill had probably killed their friends, which was why they had changed their names and moved to this tiny village. And they kept alert, watching for Hill. In case he ever found them."

"What a terrible life," said Myrna.

"When James Hill checked into the Inn and Spa, Angela recognized him and told Mike. They decided to act, before Hill could. They're claiming self-defence."

"But why did they hang him?" asked Myrna. "Wouldn't it have been easier to just knock him on the head?"

"They had to make it look like suicide. Angela had searched Hill's room while he was in Three Pines and found his suicide note. Angela had been friendly with him. Then last night she mentioned that something was wrong with her car. She hoped he'd offer to drive her home. He did. But Tom Scott almost messed it all up. Tom heard Angela say her car had broken down, and he offered to drive her. She managed to put Tom off. When they got into Hill's car, Mike was hiding in the back seat, and he strangled Hill. Mike was a big, strong guy, and Hill was older and slender. No match. Mike carried Hill through the woods, and together he and Angela got him into the tree."

"And threw him off," said Dominique. "I can't believe it of Angela. She seems so, I don't know, young."

"Yes, she seems young, almost childlike," said Gamache. "This kind of thing can happen after a terrible event. She stayed the young girl she was when the accident happened. To grow up meant to be responsible. She couldn't do that."

They sat quietly for a moment, sipping their drinks.

"I should have seen it sooner," Gamache said. "It would have been almost impossible for one person to lift Hill into that tree and hang him. The job took two people."

"What will happen to them now?" Dominique asked.

"They'll be tried for murder," said Gamache. "Their lawyer will plead self-defence."

And he might even get them off, Gamache knew. But they would never be free.